Recommendation Systems for Managers

UNLEASHING THE POWER OF DATA-DRIVEN DECISIONS

Partha Majumdar

A

Copyright © 2024 Partha Majumdar

All rights reserved.

No part of this book may be reproduced, stored in a retrieval system, or transmitted in any form or by any means, electronic, mechanical, photocopying, recording, or otherwise, without express written permission of the author.

ISBN-13: 9798322410102

Cover design by Partha Majumdar.

Unless explicitly stated, all images are created by the author or licensed from Adobe.

C

Dedicated to
Sheru and
Baghira.

Preface

In an era where data is ubiquitously hailed as the new oil, understanding how to refine this crude information into actionable insights has become a pivotal skill for managers and leaders across industries. "Recommendation Systems for Managers" is crafted to demystify the complex world of recommendation systems, making it accessible to a broad managerial audience, irrespective of their technical expertise.

This book addresses the growing need to connect recommendation systems' rapidly evolving technological landscape with businesses' practical day-to-day decision-making processes. Its goal is to equip managers, from budding to experienced, with a comprehensive understanding of how recommendation systems work, their applications, and their potential to transform business strategies.

The chapters delve into these systems' evolution, foundational principles, and industry applications.

We approach complex topics like Time Series Analysis and Market Basket Analysis with a strategic lens, minimizing the use of mathematics. Instead, we focus on the practical implications of these concepts. Real-world examples are integrated into each chapter, demonstrating the transformative power of recommendation systems in businesses.

As we explore these systems' current state and future possibilities, including their integration with technologies like AI, ML, Blockchain, AR, and VR, we invite readers to envision how they can leverage these advancements within their organizations.

"Recommendation Systems for Managers" is more than just a book; it guides forward-thinking managers eager to harness recommendation systems' potential to drive innovation, enhance customer experiences, and gain a competitive edge in the digital age.

Welcome aboard!!!

Partha Majumdar

d

e

Table of Contents

PREFACE .... B

1. **THE EVOLUTION OF RECOMMENDATION SYSTEMS 1**

   HISTORICAL CONTEXT 1
   FROM THEORY TO PRACTICE 7
   CONCLUSION 13

2. **UNDERSTANDING RECOMMENDATION SYSTEMS 15**

   BASIC CONCEPTS 15
   TYPES OF RECOMMENDATION SYSTEMS 20
   EVALUATING RECOMMENDATIONS 26
   CONCLUSION 31

3. **TIME SERIES ANALYSIS IN RECOMMENDATION SYSTEMS 33**

   CONCEPTUAL OVERVIEW 33
   REAL-LIFE EXAMPLE OF TSA IN RECOMMENDATION SYSTEMS 37
   CHALLENGES AND SOLUTIONS 41
   CONCLUSION 44

4. **LEVERAGING MARKET BASKET ANALYSIS 45**

   FUNDAMENTALS OF MARKET BASKET ANALYSIS 45
   REAL-WORLD APPLICATIONS 50
   STRATEGIC IMPLICATIONS 56
   CONCLUSION 58

5. **RECOMMENDATION SYSTEMS ACROSS INDUSTRIES .. 61**

   ENTERTAINMENT 61
   E-COMMERCE 66

f

HEALTHCARE 71
FINANCE 75
EDUCATION 80
MANAGERIAL INSIGHTS 84
CONCLUSION 86

6. THE CURRENT LANDSCAPE AND FUTURE TRENDS 87

STATE OF THE ART IN RECOMMENDATION SYSTEMS 87
INTEGRATING WITH NEW TECHNOLOGIES 92
POTENTIAL IMPACT ON BUSINESSES 98
CONCLUSION 98

7. IMPLEMENTING RECOMMENDATION SYSTEMS IN YOUR ORGANIZATION 101

GETTING STARTED WITH RECOMMENDATION SYSTEMS 101
OVERCOMING CHALLENGES 103
MEASURING SUCCESS 104
REAL-LIFE EXAMPLE: NETFLIX 106
MANAGERIAL INSIGHTS 106
CONCLUSION 107

8. ETHICAL CONSIDERATIONS AND BEST PRACTICES .. 109

ETHICAL USE OF DATA 109
MITIGATING BIAS 110
BEST PRACTICES 111
CONCLUSION 112

9. ROUNDING IT UP 115

RECAP AND REFLECTION 115
CALL TO ACTION 117
EMBRACING THE FUTURE 117

ABOUT THE AUTHOR I
    BOOKS BY THE AUTHOR II

1. The Evolution of Recommendation Systems

Historical Context

The historical trajectory of recommendation systems is a fascinating study of human interaction with technology, particularly how digital advancements have amplified and transformed our inherent desire to share and receive personalized suggestions. This narrative isn't just about algorithms and data; it's deeply entwined with the evolution of the Internet and how we interact with digital spaces.

The Genesis of Digital Recommendations

Long before the term "recommendation systems" entered the lexicon of the digital age, the concept was alive in various forms of human interaction. Imagine walking into a local bookstore, where the owner, recognizing you, suggests the latest mystery novel by your favorite author or a friend insisting you watch a film that moved them profoundly. These interactions, driven by personal knowledge and social bonds, were the precursors to today's sophisticated recommendation systems.

The digital revolution, particularly the emergence of the internet, propelled the leap from these personal, human-centric recommendations to automated, algorithm-driven systems. In its nascent stages, the Internet was a static repository of information, a one-size-fits-all model where personalization was minimal. The content was uniform, and tailoring digital experiences to individual preferences was groundbreaking and challenging.

The Pioneers of Personalization

The mid-1990s marked a pivotal moment in the history of recommendation systems, coinciding with the Internet becoming more accessible and woven into the fabric of daily life. Among the trailblazers in this domain was Amazon, a fledgling online bookstore at the time, which introduced a simple yet revolutionary feature: recommending books based on a customer's previous purchases and browsing history. This rudimentary system, a primitive form of collaborative filtering, laid the groundwork for more sophisticated recommendation algorithms.

A simple premise drove Amazon's early foray into personalized recommendations: if customers found books that effortlessly matched their interests, they were more likely to return. This profound insight shifted from static content delivery to dynamic, personalized user experiences. It wasn't just about selling more books but transforming how customers interacted with digital platforms, making these interactions more engaging, relevant, and human-centric.

The Evolution of Algorithmic Recommendations

Several critical technological advancements and landmark systems punctuate the evolution of recommendation systems. One of the most significant milestones was developing the GroupLens system in the mid-90s, which applied collaborative filtering to recommend news articles. This was soon followed by the launch of Amazon's "item-to-item collaborative filtering" in 1997, a breakthrough that significantly improved recommendation quality and personalization.

The initial success of Amazon's recommendation feature sparked a wave of interest and investment in developing more advanced algorithms capable of delivering even more personalized content. The field of collaborative filtering quickly evolved, becoming more sophisticated and capable of analyzing complex patterns of user behavior to predict what other products or content a user might enjoy.

This period saw the development of various algorithmic approaches to recommendations, each with its unique method of parsing and interpreting data to predict user preferences. These ranged from content-based filtering, which recommends items similar to what a user has liked in the past, to more complex hybrid systems that combine multiple data sources and algorithms to offer recommendations.

One of the most significant milestones in the evolution of recommendation systems was the Netflix Prize, a competition launched in 2006 by the streaming giant to improve the accuracy of its recommendation engine. The contest not only underscored the critical role of recommendation systems in retaining customer engagement but also catalyzed a surge in both academic and practical research in this field. It highlighted the growing importance of recommendation systems as a feature of e-commerce platforms and a cornerstone of the digital user experience.

The Impact of Machine Learning and AI

The advent of Machine Learning (ML) and Artificial Intelligence (AI) has significantly advanced recommendation systems, introducing a level of complexity and precision previously unattainable. Modern recommendation engines leverage these technologies to analyze vast datasets in real time, adapting to user preferences, behaviors, and even changes in mood or context.

This era of AI-driven recommendations is characterized by systems that learn from each interaction, constantly refining and improving the relevance of their suggestions. The application of deep learning algorithms has enabled the development of systems that can understand and predict user preferences with remarkable accuracy,

transforming vast arrays of data into coherent, personalized narratives.

The Social and Cultural Dimensions

As recommendation systems have become more pervasive and integral to our digital experiences, they have also raised important questions about privacy, data ethics, and the potential for algorithmic bias. These systems' ability to shape our choices, from what we read and watch to how we shop and learn, imbues them with significant social and cultural influence.

The journey of recommendation systems from manual, human-driven suggestions to sophisticated AI-powered engines is a testament to the incredible pace of technological innovation. Yet, it also serves as a reminder of the enduring value of personalization and relevance in human interactions, whether in a small bookstore or the vast expanse of the digital world. As we look to the future, the challenge will be to harness the power of these systems responsibly, ensuring they enhance rather than diminish the richness and diversity of our choices and experiences.

From Theory to Practice

The interplay between theoretical research and practical application has been a driving force in the evolution of recommendation systems. This field intersects computer science, statistics, machine learning (ML), and artificial intelligence (AI). This dynamic relationship has accelerated the development of systems capable of curating highly personalized digital experiences, marking a significant shift from the one-size-fits-all approach that characterized the early days of the Internet.

Theoretical Foundations

The theoretical underpinnings of recommendation systems are deeply rooted in academic research, drawing from a broad spectrum of disciplines. These systems use algorithms and mathematical models to predict user preferences based on past behavior and similarities among users or items. Developing these models has been a critical area of computer science and statistics, with researchers continuously exploring new methods to improve accuracy, scalability, and performance.

Collaborative filtering and content-based filtering are two foundational approaches that have emerged from this research. Collaborative filtering recommends items by finding patterns in user-item interactions. In contrast, content-based filtering suggests items similar to those a user has liked based on item features. Each method has its strengths and limitations, which has led to the exploration of hybrid models that combine aspects of both to enhance recommendation quality.

Bridging Theory and Practice

The increasing digitization of consumer behavior has facilitated the transition of recommendation systems from academic concepts to essential components of business platforms. E-commerce giants like Amazon and streaming services like Netflix and Spotify were among the first to recognize the potential of leveraging vast amounts of user data to offer personalized recommendations, enhancing user engagement and satisfaction.

These businesses have implemented theoretical models and contributed to their evolution by identifying practical challenges and limitations. For instance, the scalability of collaborative filtering algorithms was a significant concern in the early days, given the computational resources required to process large user-item matrices. Practical applications in business settings highlighted the need for more efficient algorithms, leading to innovations like matrix factorization techniques, which reduced computational complexity and improved scalability.

The Role of Machine Learning and Artificial Intelligence

The advent of machine learning and artificial intelligence has been a game-changer for recommendation systems. It has introduced the ability to process and learn from data in previously unimaginable ways. ML algorithms, particularly deep learning models, can discern intricate patterns in vast datasets, enabling systems to predict user preferences accurately.

These technologies have expanded the capabilities of recommendation systems beyond simple product suggestions. For example, personalized news feeds on social media platforms and dynamic content recommendations on streaming services are now possible, creating a highly customized user experience that adapts to user behavior and preferences changes.

AI and ML have also introduced the concept of context-aware recommendations, where the system considers the context of user interactions, such as time of day, the device used, or current location, to make more relevant suggestions. This level of personalization has significantly enhanced the user experience, making digital platforms more intuitive and responsive to individual needs.

From Products to Experiences

The evolution of recommendation systems has shifted from recommending products to curating experiences. This transition is evident in how streaming services like Netflix suggest content based on what you've watched and tailor the browsing experience, including the artwork and trailers displayed, to match your interests.

This holistic approach to personalization, where every aspect of the user interface is customized to individual preferences, exemplifies the potential of recommendation systems to transform digital platforms into unique, personalized spaces that resonate deeply with users.

Ethical Considerations and Future Directions

As recommendation systems become more sophisticated and ingrained in digital experiences, they also raise important ethical considerations. Issues related to privacy, data security, and algorithmic bias have come to the forefront, prompting a reevaluation of how these systems are designed and implemented. Ensuring transparency, fairness, and respect for user privacy has become as important as improving recommendation accuracy and personalization.

The future of recommendation systems is poised for further innovation, with emerging technologies like blockchain offering new ways to secure user data and ensure transparency. Augmented reality (AR) and virtual reality (VR) present opportunities to create even more immersive and personalized experiences, blurring the lines between digital and physical worlds.

The ongoing collaboration between academia and industry will likely continue driving advancements in this field, with each sector contributing unique insights and perspectives. As businesses seek to navigate the increasingly complex digital landscape, the role of recommendation systems in shaping user experiences and driving engagement is set to grow, making understanding these systems an essential aspect of modern management.

The journey of recommendation systems from theoretical models to integral components of business strategy underscores the dynamic nature of technological innovation. The symbiotic relationship between research and practical application has propelled the field forward, leading to systems that predict preferences and enhance the overall quality of digital interactions. As we look to the future, the challenge will be to harness these advancements responsibly, ensuring that recommendation systems continue serving the best interests of users and society.

Conclusion

The evolution of recommendation systems from simple manual suggestions to sophisticated AI-driven algorithms is a testament to the remarkable advancements in technology and data science. As we stand on the brink of breakthroughs with technologies like deep learning, blockchain, and augmented reality making their way into recommendation systems, the future promises even more personalized, intuitive, and immersive user experiences. This journey from theory to practice continues as the collaboration between academia and industry drives the relentless pursuit of better, more effective recommendation systems.

2. Understanding Recommendation Systems

In the rapidly evolving digital landscape, recommendation systems have emerged as a cornerstone technology for enhancing user experiences and driving business value. This chapter delves into the basic concepts that underpin recommendation systems, their primary types, and the methodologies employed to evaluate their effectiveness. By focusing on the practical applications of these systems, this discussion aims to provide managers with a comprehensive understanding of how recommendation systems can be leveraged to achieve strategic objectives, irrespective of their technical background.

Basic Concepts

Recommendation systems have revolutionized how digital platforms interact with users by delivering personalized content, products, or services. These systems emphasize personalization, user profiling, and item cataloging to enhance user engagement and satisfaction. By understanding these fundamental concepts, businesses can create more engaging and user-friendly digital experiences.

Personalization

Personalization is the cornerstone of recommendation systems. It aims to deliver a unique and tailored experience to each user. It leverages data on user preferences, behaviors, and interactions with the system to make relevant suggestions.

1. **Streaming Services**: Netflix, a streaming giant, excels in personalization by recommending movies and TV shows based on users' viewing histories and the ratings they've provided. By analyzing these data points, Netflix creates a personalized "For You" list, ensuring users are presented with content that aligns with their tastes, thus increasing engagement and time spent on the platform.
2. **E-Commerce Platforms**: Amazon utilizes personalization to enhance the shopping experience. It analyzes past purchase history, items in the shopping cart, and what other

customers have viewed or purchased to suggest products that a user might be interested in. This simplifies the shopping process and increases the likelihood of user purchases by presenting tailored options that match individual preferences.

User Profiles

User profiles are digital representations of users' preferences and interests compiled from accumulated data. These profiles are dynamic, evolving with each user interaction, which makes the recommendations increasingly accurate.

1. **Social Media Platforms**: Facebook creates comprehensive user profiles by tracking interactions such as likes, shares, comments, and time spent on different posts. These profiles help Facebook's recommendation system suggest relevant content, friend connections, and advertisements, creating a more engaging social media experience tailored to individual users' interests.
2. **Online News Portals**: Using user profiles, news portals like The New York Times tailor the

news feed and article recommendations. The system can recommend similar content by analyzing which articles users read, share, or spend the most time on. This ensures that users are more likely to engage with the news feed, which resonates with their interests and reading habits.

Item Cataloging

Item cataloging involves tagging each item with attributes or features that describe it. This detailed understanding of items allows the system to match them with user profiles, recommending items that users are likely to find appealing.

1. **Music Streaming Services**: Spotify catalogs songs and albums with various attributes, including genre, mood, tempo, and artist. This detailed cataloging allows Spotify's recommendation system to curate personalized playlists such as "Discover Weekly," which introduces users to new music that aligns with their listening history and preferences, thus enhancing user satisfaction and discovery.

2. **Online Retailers**: Online retailers, such as Zappos, catalog their products by size, color, style, brand, and more. This extensive item cataloging enables Zappos to recommend products that closely match what a user has searched for or previously purchased. For example, if a user frequently purchases running shoes, Zappos can recommend new arrivals or popular products within that specific category, increasing the likelihood of further purchases.

In Summary

By leveraging these core concepts, recommendation systems can significantly enhance users' digital experience. Personalization ensures that each user feels valued and understood, leading to increased engagement. User profiles allow the system to continuously learn and adapt to changing preferences, ensuring the recommendations remain relevant. Lastly, item cataloging provides the foundation for matching user preferences with the right products or content, making the recommendation process more efficient and effective.

The interplay of personalization, user profiles, and item cataloging within recommendation systems offers businesses a powerful tool for engaging with their audience on a deeper level. By creating personalized experiences that resonate with individual users, companies can foster loyalty, increase user satisfaction, and ultimately drive business growth. As these systems continue to evolve, they will play an increasingly pivotal role in shaping the future of digital interactions, making understanding their underlying principles essential for managers and professionals across industries.

Types of Recommendation Systems

Recommendation systems are broadly categorized into collaborative filtering, content-based filtering, and hybrid systems, each offering unique advantages and applications.

Collaborative Filtering

Collaborative filtering, one of the most widely used recommendation techniques, generates suggestions based on similar users' preferences. This method operates on the premise that users are likely to agree again if they agreed on specific items in the past.

- **User-Based Collaborative Filtering**: User-based collaborative filtering identifies user similarities based on their ratings or interactions with items. Recommendations are then made to a user based on the preferences of other users with similar tastes.
  - **Movie Recommendations**: A classic implementation of user-based collaborative filtering is seen in movie streaming platforms like Netflix. If User A and User B have highly rated similar movies in the past, and User B rates a new movie highly, that movie may be recommended to User A, assuming they will also enjoy it.
  - **Social Networking Sites**: LinkedIn uses user-based collaborative filtering to suggest professional connections. If User A is connected to Users B and C, and Users B and C are both connected to User D, LinkedIn might suggest User

D as a potential connection to User A, based on the shared network.
- **Item-based Collaborative Filtering**: In contrast, item-based collaborative filtering focuses on the relationships between items rather than users. It recommends items similar to those a user has liked or interacted with previously.
  - **E-Commerce Websites**: Amazon employs item-based collaborative filtering for product recommendations. If a user purchases or views a particular book, Amazon recommends other books that customers bought or viewed alongside the original item, assuming they share similar attributes or themes.
  - **Music Streaming Services**: Spotify uses item-based collaborative filtering for its "You Might Also Like" feature. Suppose a user frequently listens to songs from a specific artist. In that case, Spotify recommends other songs that fans of the artist also listen to, leveraging the similarity in musical taste among its user bases.

Content-Based Filtering

Content-based filtering diverges from collaborative approaches by focusing on the items' attributes. It recommends items by comparing the features of a user's previously liked items to those not yet encountered.

- **News Aggregators**: News aggregators like Flipboard use content-based filtering to personalize news feeds. If a user frequently reads technology articles, Flipboard will recommend other technology-related articles, utilizing keywords and topics to find similar content.
- **Online Bookstores**: Online bookstores, such as Goodreads, recommend books by analyzing the genres, authors, and themes of books a user has rated highly. If a user enjoys mystery novels by a particular author, Goodreads might suggest other books within the mystery genre or works by the same author.

Hybrid Systems

Hybrid systems combine collaborative and content-based filtering strengths to overcome their respective limitations and improve recommendation quality.

- **Streaming Platforms**: Netflix is known for its sophisticated recommendation engine, a hybrid system. It combines user behavior (collaborative filtering) with content analysis (content-based filtering) to recommend movies and TV shows. This approach allows Netflix to make accurate recommendations by considering the users' similarities and the content's characteristics.
- **E-Commerce Personalization**: E-commerce platforms like Alibaba use hybrid recommendation systems to enhance user experience. They blend collaborative filtering to capture user behavior patterns and content-based filtering to analyze product details, ensuring that recommendations are relevant to the user's interests and similar to items they've engaged with.

Hybrid systems represent the forefront of recommendation technology, offering a balanced approach that maximizes the relevancy and diversity of suggestions. By leveraging multiple data sources and algorithms, these systems provide a comprehensive solution to personalizing user experiences in a complex digital environment.

In summary

Understanding the nuances and applications of collaborative filtering, content-based filtering, and hybrid systems is crucial for managers looking to implement recommendation systems in their operations. Each type offers distinct advantages and can be tailored to meet specific business needs, ensuring users receive personalized, relevant, and engaging content. As digital platforms continue to evolve, the role of sophisticated recommendation systems in shaping user experiences and driving engagement will only grow, highlighting the importance of these technologies in the modern digital landscape.

Evaluating Recommendations

Evaluating the efficacy of recommendation systems is paramount in ensuring they serve their intended purpose: to enhance user engagement and satisfaction by providing personalized and relevant suggestions. The assessment of these systems revolves around several key metrics, each offering insights into different facets of performance. This comprehensive evaluation not only measures the system's current effectiveness but also guides future enhancements and adjustments.

Precision in Recommendations

Precision is a critical metric in recommendation systems, representing the accuracy of the user-provided suggestions. It is defined as the ratio of relevant items recommended to the total number of items recommended. High precision indicates that a significant proportion of the items suggested by the system are of interest to the user, affirming the system's effectiveness in understanding and catering to individual preferences.

- **Online Retail Platforms**: Consider an online retail platform recommending products based on users' browsing history. If a user browses through ten products and the system recommends five, but the user finds only three relevant or appealing, the precision of the recommendation is 60% (3 relevant recommendations out of 5 total recommendations). This metric helps the platform understand how well its recommendations align with user interests, guiding adjustments to improve recommendation relevance.
- **Movie Streaming Services**: Precision is vital in keeping users engaged in a movie streaming service. If a system suggests ten movies to a user, and the user watches and enjoys seven of them, the precision is 70%. This high precision indicates the system's success in predicting the user's movie preferences, leading to increased user satisfaction and platform engagement.

Recall in Recommendations

Recall complements precision by measuring the system's ability to identify all relevant items for the user. It is the ratio of relevant items recommended to the total number of relevant items available. High recall indicates that the system effectively uncovers a broad spectrum of items that align with the user's interests, enhancing the discovery experience.

- **Music Recommendation Engines**: A music streaming service uses a recommendation engine to suggest new songs to users. If 100 songs align with a user's taste in the database, and the system recommends 80%, the recall is 80%. This high recall rate ensures that users are exposed to a wide array of music they are likely to enjoy, enriching their listening experience and potentially increasing platform loyalty.

- **Academic Journals and Articles**: Recall is significant in academic databases for researchers seeking comprehensive literature. Suppose a recommendation system can surface 95% of all relevant articles from a vast database. In that case, it significantly aids researchers in their literature review process, ensuring they have access to a broad and relevant body of work.

User Satisfaction

User satisfaction transcends quantitative metrics like precision and recall, capturing users' subjective experience and overall satisfaction with the recommendation system. It can be gauged through direct feedback, such as ratings and reviews of the recommendations, or indirectly through engagement metrics like click-through rates, time spent on recommended items, and retention rates.

- **E-commerce Customer Reviews**: An e-commerce platform may allow users to rate the usefulness of product recommendations. Positive reviews and high ratings indicate that users find the recommendations valuable, reflecting high user satisfaction. This qualitative feedback is crucial for understanding the personal impact of recommendations on the shopping experience.

- **Content Platforms and Engagement Metrics:** For content platforms like news aggregators or blogs, user engagement metrics provide valuable insights into satisfaction. High click-through rates on recommended articles, increased time spent reading suggested content, and a lower bounce rate indicate a recommendation system that successfully captures and holds users' interests, contributing to overall satisfaction.

Balancing Precision, Recall, and User Satisfaction

The goal of a recommendation system is to achieve a harmonious balance between precision, recall, and user satisfaction. High precision ensures the recommendations are relevant, while high recall guarantees a comprehensive discovery experience. However, maximizing both can be challenging, as improving one often comes at the expense of the other. User satisfaction is the overarching metric encompassing the user experience's subjective quality, influenced by precision and recall.

Achieving this balance requires continuous monitoring and adjustment of the recommendation algorithms. A/B testing, user feedback mechanisms, and engagement analytics play pivotal roles in this iterative process allowing system developers and managers to fine-tune the system to meet user needs better.

Conclusion

Understanding the basic principles, types, and evaluation methods of recommendation systems is essential for managers looking to harness the power of personalized suggestions in their digital platforms. By focusing on personalization, user profiles, item cataloging, and choosing the right recommendation system, managers can significantly enhance user engagement and satisfaction, driving business growth.

3. Time Series Analysis in Recommendation Systems

In the dynamic world of digital platforms, understanding and predicting user behavior over time is crucial for maintaining engagement and delivering personalized experiences. Time Series Analysis (TSA) is a powerful tool in this context, particularly when integrated into recommendation systems. This chapter delves into the conceptual framework of TSA, its applications in enhancing recommendation systems, and the challenges and strategies associated with its implementation.

Conceptual Overview

Time series analysis involves the study of data points collected or sequenced at specific time intervals. In recommendation systems, TSA is employed to discern patterns, trends, and cyclical behaviors within user interaction data over time. This analysis can unveil temporal dynamics in user preferences, allowing for more nuanced and timely recommendations.

At its core, TSA is about observing how specific metrics evolve. It's like watching the tide change at the beach; just as you might predict the tide's rise and fall based on past patterns, TSA helps predict future user behaviors based on historical data. This predictive capability is invaluable in recommendation systems that aim to stay one step ahead of user needs.

For instance, a user's interaction with an e-commerce platform might reveal a penchant for purchasing certain types of products during specific seasons or holidays. By analyzing these temporal patterns, a recommendation system can anticipate user needs and preferences at different times, offering more relevant suggestions.

Amazon has long utilized sophisticated recommendation algorithms to enhance user experience. A notable instance is during the holiday season, particularly around Christmas. Amazon's recommendation system, powered by extensive data analysis, including time series analysis, observed a recurring increase in the sales of historical fiction books during December across several years. This trend could be attributed to people buying gifts for friends and family and individuals purchasing books for holiday reading.

Recognizing this pattern, Amazon's recommendation system prioritized and suggested historical fiction titles more prominently to users during the holiday season. This strategic alignment of recommendations with observed seasonal preferences improved user experience by providing more relevant suggestions and contributed to an increase in sales of historical fiction books during December.

Amazon's adept use of time series analysis to inform its recommendation system demonstrates the practical application and benefits of understanding temporal patterns in user behavior. By aligning recommendations with seasonal trends, Amazon ensures that users are presented with products that match their interests and needs, enhancing the overall shopping experience.

Another example involves Spotify, the widely used music streaming service. Spotify leverages its vast user data collection and sophisticated algorithms, including time series analysis, to enhance its recommendation system. A specific event illustrating this is Spotify's launch of the "Spotify Wrapped"

feature, which becomes available at the end of each year.

"Spotify Wrapped" compiles personalized insights and statistics about users' listening habits over the past year, including top songs, artists, genres, and total listening time. This feature reflects users' past preferences and cleverly uses this data to recommend new playlists and artists that align with these trends. For example, suppose the data reveals a significant uptick in the listening of electronic dance music (EDM) during summer months across the user base. In that case, Spotify's recommendation system might prioritize EDM tracks and artists in user recommendations during this season in subsequent years.

The success of "Spotify Wrapped" is a testament to how effectively analyzing temporal patterns in user behavior can enhance engagement and satisfaction. By recognizing and leveraging seasonal trends in music listening, Spotify can offer more targeted and timely recommendations, enriching the user experience and reassuring you that your music journey is in good hands.

Real-Life Example of TSA in Recommendation Systems

Let us discuss more real-life applications of TSA in industry recommendation systems to appreciate its importance.

Predicting Seasonal Product Popularity

Understanding and predicting seasonal trends can significantly enhance inventory management and marketing strategies in the retail sector. For example, an online clothing retailer might use TSA to analyze historical sales data and identify that lightweight apparel sales spike in the spring and summer months. Leveraging this insight, the recommendation system can proactively suggest seasonal attire to users, aligning with anticipated needs and preferences.

In e-commerce, TSA plays a pivotal role in aligning product recommendations with seasonal trends. Take, for instance, a gardening supplies website. Through TSA, the site might identify that interest in garden hoses peaks in spring, while snow shovels see a surge in winter. With this knowledge, the recommendation system can dynamically adjust its suggestions to match seasonal demand, offering garden hoses in March and snow shovels in November, enhancing relevance and user satisfaction.

Airbnb utilizes TSA to optimize its property recommendations. By analyzing booking trends, the platform might discover that beachfront properties in Miami are highly sought-after during winter, while mountain cabins in Colorado are popular in summer. This insight allows Airbnb to tailor its recommendations based on the time of year, highlighting beach properties in December and mountain retreats in July, significantly improving user experience by aligning recommendations with seasonal preferences.

Netflix, a leader in the streaming industry, leverages TSA to analyze viewing patterns and offer recommendations that align with seasonal trends and holidays. For instance, during Halloween, Netflix leverages increased interest in horror and thriller genres. By recognizing this trend, Netflix's recommendation system highlights spooky series and movies, such as "Stranger Things" or "The Haunting of Hill House," making it easier for users to find content that matches the seasonal mood.

User Activity Trends

Streaming platforms like Netflix or Spotify apply TSA to user interaction data to discern viewing or listening patterns at different times. Spotify, a prime example, uses TSA to curate personalized playlists with remarkable accuracy. By analyzing your listening habits over time, Spotify can discern that you prefer upbeat pop songs on Friday evenings and mellow acoustic tracks on Sunday mornings. This temporal pattern enables Spotify's recommendation system to suggest a "Friday Night Party" playlist at the end of the week and a "Lazy Sunday Morning" playlist on weekends, perfectly resonating with your mood at those specific times.

YouTube, the world's largest video-sharing platform, uses TSA to track the popularity of videos over time. This analysis allows YouTube to identify viral trends and emerging topics. For example, during major global events like the FIFA World Cup, YouTube's recommendation system prioritizes football-related content, match highlights, and fan reactions, tapping into the heightened interest around the event. This timely and relevant curation keeps users engaged and ensures they don't miss out on trending content.

Peloton, known for its interactive fitness platform, applies TSA to optimize workout recommendations. By analyzing workout completion data, Peloton finds that users prefer high-intensity interval training (HIIT) sessions during weekday mornings and more relaxed, yoga-based workouts on weekends. With this insight, Peloton's recommendation system can suggest appropriate classes that fit users' preferred workout intensity for specific times, enhancing the overall fitness experience.

Audible, a popular audiobook service, utilizes TSA to understand listening habits. The service notices an increased consumption of motivational and business-related audiobooks during weekdays, possibly during commuting hours, and a preference for fiction and leisure reading on weekends. By tailoring recommendations according to these patterns, Audible ensures that users can access content that suits their mood and available time, making the service more valuable and engaging.

In Summary

Time Series Analysis (TSA) is crucial in tailoring user experiences on digital platforms. These examples recommendation systems can incorporate adaptive models that rely on historical data and factor in real-time signals from social media, news trends, or even global events to adjust recommendations accordingly.

Balancing Timeliness with Relevance

While TSA provides a temporal dimension to recommendations, ensuring these suggestions remain relevant to the individual user is crucial. This involves leveraging historical patterns and incorporating user interactions and feedback. Adaptive algorithms that analyze historical trends and recent user behavior are essential to maintaining this balance.

Privacy and Data Security

As TSA often involves analyzing detailed user interaction data over time, it raises significant privacy and data security concerns. Ensuring compliance with data protection regulations (like GDPR) and implementing stringent data security measures is paramount. Anonymizing data and employing encryption can protect user privacy while allowing meaningful analysis.

Conclusion

Time series analysis offers a valuable perspective for recommendation systems, allowing them to capture the temporal dimensions of user behavior and preferences. By integrating TSA, these systems can make more contextually aware and timely recommendations, significantly enhancing user experience. However, implementing TSA is challenging, requiring careful consideration of data management, analysis techniques, and privacy concerns. As recommendation systems evolve, the integration of time series analysis will likely play an increasingly central role, driven by the ongoing quest for deeper personalization and relevance in user recommendations.

4. Leveraging Market Basket Analysis

Market Basket Analysis (MBA) emerges as a pivotal tool in the intricate landscape of recommendation systems, particularly within the retail and e-commerce sectors. This chapter unfolds the fundamentals of the MBA, showcases its real-world applications, and elucidates the strategic implications it holds for managers aiming to refine customer experiences and boost sales through intelligent cross-selling and upselling strategies.

Fundamentals of Market Basket Analysis

Market Basket Analysis (MBA) is a compelling data mining technique widely employed in retail to discover associations between items. It analyzes transaction data to identify patterns of items frequently bought together. MBA is instrumental in recommendation systems, guiding cross-selling and upselling strategies by unveiling product affinities that might not be intuitively apparent. This analysis hinges on association rule learning, a method that uncovers how the occurrence of one item in a transaction implies the presence of another.

Understanding Association Rules

Association rules are expressed in the form of "If {A}, then {B}," where A and B are distinct items or sets of items. The strength and reliability of these rules are evaluated using metrics such as support, confidence, and lift, each providing different insights into the rule's usefulness and relevance.

Support

Support measures the frequency or proportion of transactions that include a specific item or combination of items within the dataset. It reflects how frequently items appear together and is crucial for identifying significant associations worth further exploration.

For instance, if a retail database has 1,000 transactions and 100 of these include bread and butter, the support for the rule "If bread, then butter" is calculated as 100/1,000 or 10%. A higher support value indicates a stronger rule, suggesting that the item association is not random but a common pattern among transactions.

Confidence

Confidence assesses the likelihood of item B being purchased when item A is bought. It's calculated by dividing the number of transactions containing both A and B by the number of transactions containing A. Confidence thus measures the reliability of a rule's inference.

Taking the previous example, if 200 of the 1,000 transactions include bread, the confidence for the rule "If bread, then butter" would be 100/200 or 50%. This suggests that given that a transaction includes bread, there's a 50% chance it will also include butter.

Lift

Lift evaluates the strength of an association by comparing how often items A and B are purchased together with how often they would be purchased together if they were statistically independent. It's calculated by dividing the rule's confidence by the support of the consequent item (B) in all transactions. A lift value greater than 1 indicates that items A and B are more likely to be bought together than separately, suggesting a positive association.

Continuing with the bread-and-butter example, if butter appears in 150 out of 1,000 transactions, the lift of the rule "If bread, then butter" would be (0.5 / 150/1,000) or 3.33. This indicates that bread and butter are over three times more likely to be bought together than expected if independent, highlighting a strong association.

Real-World Application of MBA Metrics

These MBA metrics can provide actionable insights for businesses. For example, an e-commerce platform could use MBA to analyze user purchase history. By identifying strong rules with high support and confidence, the platform can recommend products users will likely buy based on their current shopping cart contents. Lift can help distinguish genuinely interesting associations from those that occur simply due to the popularity of certain items.

Technical Considerations and Challenges

Implementing MBA involves several technical considerations, particularly in handling large datasets. Efficient algorithms such as the Apriori or FP-Growth algorithm are often used to manage computational complexity by iteratively reducing the itemsets under consideration. Moreover, the choice of threshold values for support, confidence, and lift significantly impacts the quality and quantity of rules generated. Setting these thresholds too low might result in an overwhelming number of trivial associations, while values that are too high might miss out on valuable insights.

MBA is about generating rules and interpreting them to make informed business decisions. For instance, a supermarket might use MBA insights to layout the store more effectively, placing items with strong associations near each other to encourage additional purchases. Online retailers can personalize user experiences by dynamically adjusting product recommendations based on the shopping cart's current contents, leveraging MBA insights to enhance the likelihood of additional purchases.

Market Basket Analysis offers a robust framework for understanding item associations within transactional data. MBA provides a quantitative basis for uncovering patterns that can inform strategic business decisions by employing metrics like support, confidence, and lift. Whether in physical retail environments or online platforms, leveraging MBA can significantly enhance recommendation systems, improve customer satisfaction, increase sales through effective cross-selling and upselling, and a deeper understanding of customer purchasing behavior. As businesses continue to navigate an increasingly data-driven landscape, the strategic application of MBA in recommendation systems will undoubtedly play a pivotal role in shaping competitive advantage and driving growth.

Real-World Applications

Market Basket Analysis (MBA) extends beyond mere transactional analysis, transforming retail and e-commerce landscapes by uncovering deep product associations. Through its insightful revelations, MBA enables businesses to implement strategic cross-selling and upselling, elevating the customer experience to new heights and significantly bolstering sales.

Retail Sector: Cross-Selling in Supermarkets

Market Basket Analysis (MBA) is a powerful tool in the retail sector, particularly in supermarkets where the diversity of products offers ample opportunities for cross-selling. By analyzing transaction data, supermarkets can uncover patterns indicating which products are frequently bought together and use these insights to optimize store layout and promotions, ultimately enhancing the customer shopping experience and increasing sales.

For instance, an MBA might reveal a strong association between pasta, pasta sauce, and parmesan cheese, suggesting that customers buying one item are likely to purchase the others during the same shopping trip. This association is not merely coincidental but reflects a typical usage pattern, combining these items to prepare a meal.

With this knowledge, a supermarket can employ several strategies to capitalize on the identified association. One practical approach is to place these items near each other in the store. This strategic placement ensures that customers looking for pasta are immediately reminded of or introduced to complementary products like sauce and cheese, making it convenient for them to pick up all the necessary ingredients for their meal in one go. Such an arrangement enhances the shopping experience by significantly reducing the time and effort required to locate related items. It also encourages the purchase of additional products, thereby increasing the transaction value.

The supermarket can leverage these insights by creating targeted marketing campaigns or promotions. For example, they could discount parmesan cheese when bought with a specific brand of pasta and sauce or create bundled offers for all three items at a slightly reduced price. These promotions incentivize additional purchases and help introduce customers to products they might not have considered otherwise, potentially leading to new buying habits and a significant boost in sales and revenue.

Furthermore, understanding these product associations enables supermarkets to manage inventory more effectively. Knowing that certain

products are likely to be bought together can help forecast demand more accurately, ensuring that these items are adequately stocked, especially during peak shopping or promotional periods.

By applying MBA to uncover product associations, supermarkets can significantly enhance the shopping experience through thoughtful store layouts and targeted promotions. This not only simplifies the customer journey, making it more likely that they will find everything they need in one trip, but also strategically encourages the purchase of additional items. As a result, supermarkets can see increased customer satisfaction and loyalty, positively impacting sales and revenue.

E-commerce Platforms: Personalized Recommendations

Amazon, a pioneer in the e-commerce industry, has redefined the online shopping experience through strategic data analytics, notably Market Basket Analysis (MBA). A prime example is Amazon's "Customers who bought this item also bought" feature, demonstrating how MBA can be leveraged to offer personalized recommendations, enhance user experience, and drive sales.

At the heart of this feature lies a complex algorithm that sifts through vast amounts of transaction data to identify patterns and associations between products. When a customer views a product, say a smartphone, Amazon's recommendation system quickly analyzes historical purchase data to find other items frequently bought together with the smartphone. This might include complementary products such as cases, screen protectors, and charging accessories, which are then presented to the customer as recommendations.

The personalized recommendation approach is designed to simplify the shopping process for customers. By suggesting accessories and related products that customers might need but haven't considered, Amazon enhances the shopping experience. This convenience factor significantly increases the likelihood of customers completing a purchase and returning to the platform.

Secondly, by showcasing complementary products, Amazon encourages additional purchases, increasing the average transaction value. A customer initially intending to buy just a smartphone might add a case or screen protector to their cart, driven by the convenience of finding these recommended products directly on the product page.

These personalized recommendations are not static; they constantly evolve based on real-time data and changing customer behavior patterns. This dynamic approach ensures that the recommendations are always up-to-date and relevant, increasing their effectiveness.

The strategic placement of these recommendations, often on the product page or during the checkout process, capitalizes on the customer's existing purchase intent, making it more likely that they will consider these additional items. Furthermore, this feature also introduces customers to a broader range of products they might not have discovered independently, enhancing product visibility and potentially leading to new purchasing trends.

Amazon's use of MBA for personalized recommendations exemplifies a data-driven strategy that aligns closely with customer needs and preferences. This leads to a more satisfying shopping experience and drives incremental sales, showcasing the profound impact of advanced data analytics in the e-commerce sector. As e-commerce continues to evolve, the role of sophisticated analytical tools like MBA in shaping personalized shopping experiences will undoubtedly grow, setting new benchmarks for customer engagement and business success in the digital marketplace.

Strategic Implications

Exploring the strategic implications of Market Basket Analysis (MBA) reveals its profound impact beyond mere item associations. MBA influences cross-selling, upselling, customer experience, and supply chain management. Its insights empower managers to devise nuanced strategies, enhancing business operations and customer satisfaction.

Enhancing Cross-Selling Opportunities

Understanding item associations allows managers to craft strategic cross-selling opportunities, increasing the average transaction value. For example, an online electronics retailer, armed with insights from MBA, might bundle cameras with tripods and memory cards at a special price, enticing customers to make additional purchases that they perceive as value-adding.

Refining Upselling Tactics

MBA can also inform upselling strategies by identifying higher-value items or upgrades commonly chosen by customers. A software company, for instance, could use an MBA to determine that businesses purchasing the basic CRM package often upgrade to a premium version within six months. This insight enables targeted marketing campaigns to educate customers about the premium package's benefits, potentially accelerating the upselling process.

Improving Customer Experience

Beyond sales strategies, MBA's insights contribute to a more personalized and satisfying shopping experience. By understanding item associations, retailers can design their online platforms and physical stores to mirror customer behavior, making it easier for customers to find related products. This thoughtful organization enhances the customer's journey, increasing satisfaction and loyalty.

Inventory and Supply Chain Optimization

MBA also plays a crucial role in inventory management and supply chain optimization. By predicting item associations and understanding purchasing patterns, managers can better forecast demand for products and their complements, ensuring optimal stock levels and reducing the risk of stockouts or overstock situations.

Conclusion

Market Basket Analysis is more than a tool for uncovering item associations; it is a strategic asset that can significantly enhance recommendation systems, driving sales through effective cross-selling and upselling while simultaneously elevating the customer experience. Managers equipped with the insights provided by MBA can make informed decisions that boost the bottom line and foster customer loyalty through personalized, convenient shopping experiences. As the retail and e-commerce landscapes continue to evolve, the application of MBA in recommendation systems will undoubtedly become even more sophisticated, playing a central role in shaping future shopping experiences.

5. Recommendation Systems Across Industries

In the digital age, recommendation systems have become indispensable across various industries, enhancing user experience and driving business growth. This chapter delves into the diverse applications of recommendation systems, presenting success stories from entertainment to healthcare, and provides actionable insights for managers looking to adopt these systems.

Entertainment

In the dynamic realm of entertainment, recommendation systems have emerged as a cornerstone technology, profoundly transforming how content is curated and consumed. The exponential growth of digital content platforms like Netflix and Spotify has led to an information overload, making the role of efficient recommendation systems more critical than ever. These systems harness sophisticated algorithms to sift through vast content libraries, providing users with personalized recommendations that align with their unique preferences and habits.

The Mechanism Behind Recommendation Systems

At the heart of these recommendation systems in entertainment platforms are complex algorithms that leverage user data to predict preferences. These systems analyze various data points, including viewing history, ratings provided, search queries, and even the time spent on specific titles. Advanced machine learning models and techniques such as collaborative filtering, content-based filtering, and hybrid approaches are employed to process this data.

For instance, collaborative filtering analyzes content consumption patterns across multiple users to recommend content enjoyed by others with similar tastes. In contrast, content-based filtering focuses on the attributes of the content itself, recommending similar types of movies, shows, or music that a user has previously enjoyed. Hybrid models combine both approaches to enhance the accuracy and relevance of recommendations.

Personalization: The Key to User Engagement

The success of recommendation systems in the entertainment industry lies in their ability to personalize the user experience. Netflix, for example, offers a list of popular shows and a curated "For You" list that reflects individual user's preferences, ensuring that even niche titles find their audience. This level of personalization keeps users engaged, significantly reducing the chances of churn and enhancing the overall platform value.

Spotify's "Discover Weekly" is another exemplary case of personalized content delivery. This feature provides users with a weekly playlist of songs tailored to their music tastes, often including tracks they haven't heard but are likely to enjoy. This keeps users returning for more and fosters the discovery of new artists and genres, enriching the user's music experience.

Bridging Content and User Preferences

The bridge between vast content libraries and individual user preferences built by recommendation systems is about keeping users engaged and creating a meaningful connection between users and content. These systems can uncover hidden patterns and preferences by analyzing user behavior and content characteristics, often surprising users with content they might not have discovered.

For example, a user who predominantly watches sci-fi movies might be recommended a documentary on space exploration, subtly broadening their viewing horizon while staying within the realm of their interests. Similarly, a Spotify user who listens to classical music might find a contemporary piece influenced by classical elements in their recommended list, gently introducing them to modern interpretations of their preferred genre.

The Challenge of Balancing Diversity and Relevance

One significant challenge recommendation systems face in the entertainment sector is balancing diversity and relevance. While it's essential to cater to a user's established preferences, it's equally crucial to introduce variety and prevent the "filter bubble" effect, where users are only exposed to content that closely matches their past behavior.

Platforms address this challenge by incorporating elements of randomness and exploring user interactions in their recommendation algorithms. This ensures that while the recommendations remain relevant, they include unexpected yet potentially exciting content. This approach enhances content discovery and keeps the user experience fresh and engaging.

Ethical Considerations and Future Directions

As recommendation systems become increasingly integral to the entertainment industry, ethical considerations surrounding user data privacy and algorithmic transparency have emerged. It is paramount to ensure that user data is used responsibly and that recommendations do not perpetuate biases or misinformation.

The future of recommendation systems in entertainment is likely to see even more sophisticated AI models, incorporating natural language processing and sentiment analysis to understand user reviews and feedback better. Integrating virtual reality (VR) and augmented reality (AR) content into recommendation algorithms could provide more immersive and personalized entertainment experiences.

E-commerce

In e-commerce, recommendation systems have become integral to the digital shopping experience, revolutionizing how products are discovered, displayed, and purchased online. Giants in the field, such as Amazon, have been at the forefront of employing these systems to enhance user engagement, personalize shopping experiences, and drive sales by increasing the average order value through effective cross-selling and upselling strategies.

The Backbone of E-commerce Recommendation Systems

The underlying mechanism of e-commerce recommendation systems involves complex algorithms that analyze vast amounts of data related to user behavior, including past purchases, search queries, product views, and even items left in the shopping cart. This data is then processed using machine learning techniques to identify patterns, preferences, and potential interests unique to each user.

Two primary methods utilized in these systems are collaborative filtering and content-based filtering. Collaborative filtering draws on the behavior of similar users to recommend products, operating under the premise that if users A and B have identical shopping patterns, then the products liked by A would likely appeal to B as well. Conversely, content-based filtering recommends products similar to those the user has shown interest in before, focusing on their product characteristics.

Enhancing User Experience Through Personalization

The power of recommendation systems in e-commerce lies in their ability to offer highly personalized shopping experiences. For instance, when users visit Amazon, they are greeted with a homepage that reflects their interests, from product recommendations to tailored deals and promotions. This personalization makes the shopping experience more relevant and engaging for the user, increasing the likelihood of purchase.

Moreover, these systems enable dynamic product discovery, where users are introduced to items they might need but are unaware of. This aspect is particularly beneficial in cross-selling, where complementary products are suggested. For example, a user purchasing a camera might receive recommendations for compatible lenses, memory cards, or carrying cases, encouraging additional purchases that enhance the primary product's value.

Upselling: Guiding Users to Better Choices

Upselling is another area where recommendation systems excel. They guide users towards premium products or newer models that offer more features or better value. By analyzing user interactions and purchase history, these systems can identify opportunities to suggest upgrades or higher-end alternatives at critical decision points, such as when a user is viewing a product or about to check out.

For example, a user browsing entry-level smartphones on an e-commerce platform might be shown a side-by-side comparison with a slightly more expensive model offering significant feature improvements. This comparison, presented at the right moment, can convince the user of the better model's value, leading to a higher-value purchase.

Beyond Sales: Building Long-Term Customer Relationships

While increasing sales is a primary goal, e-commerce recommendation systems also play a crucial role in building and maintaining long-term customer relationships. These systems enhance customer satisfaction and loyalty by consistently providing relevant and timely product suggestions. Users are more likely to return to a platform that understands their needs and makes their shopping experience convenient and enjoyable.

Furthermore, recommendation systems' data collected and analyzed offer valuable insights into consumer behavior, preferences, and emerging trends. E-commerce businesses can use this information to optimize their inventory, marketing strategies, and overall business decisions, aligning more closely with customer expectations and market demands.

Ethical Considerations and Future Directions

As recommendation systems evolve, ethical considerations, particularly regarding data privacy and user consent, have become increasingly important. Ensuring transparency in collecting, using, and protecting user data is vital to maintaining user trust and complying with regulatory standards.

Looking ahead, the integration of advanced technologies like AI and natural language processing promises to make e-commerce recommendation systems even more sophisticated and intuitive. Future systems could offer even more personalized experiences by understanding user reviews and feedback in natural language, predicting emerging trends, and adapting to real-time market changes.

Healthcare

In the evolving healthcare landscape, the integration of recommendation systems is beginning to play a pivotal role in transforming patient care, diagnosis, and treatment processes. Leveraging vast amounts of data, these systems offer the potential to personalize healthcare at an unprecedented scale, tailoring treatments, medications, and care plans to each patient's unique needs.

Personalization in Patient Care

The cornerstone of modern healthcare recommendation systems is the ability to provide personalized care. By analyzing patient history, genetic information, lifestyle factors, and data from similar cases, these systems can suggest customized treatment plans that are more likely to be effective for the individual patient. This level of personalization increases the efficacy of treatments and enhances patient satisfaction and engagement with their care plans.

For instance, in oncology, recommendation systems can analyze the genetic makeup of a patient's tumor, compare it with vast databases of similar cases, and recommend a treatment plan that has shown the highest success rate for that specific genetic profile. This approach, known as precision medicine, marks a significant departure from the one-size-fits-all strategy, leading to improved outcomes and reduced side effects.

Enhancing Diagnosis and Treatment

Recommendation systems in healthcare can also assist in the diagnostic process by suggesting potential diagnoses based on symptoms, lab results, and patient history. This can be particularly valuable in complex cases where the diagnosis is not straightforward. By drawing on historical data and the latest medical research, these systems can help healthcare providers consider a broader range of possibilities and make more informed decisions.

Furthermore, in treatment selection, recommendation systems can suggest medications and dosages tailored to the patient's profile, considering factors like age, weight, comorbidities, and even genetic factors that might affect drug metabolism. This targeted approach helps minimize trial and error, reduce the risk of adverse drug reactions, and optimize treatment efficacy.

Streamlining Healthcare Resource Utilization

Another area where recommendation systems can profoundly impact the efficient use of healthcare resources is resource allocation. By predicting patient flows, these systems can help allocate resources, ensuring facilities are adequately staffed and equipped to handle patient volumes. This can lead to reduced wait times, improved patient care, and optimized operational efficiency.

In chronic disease management, recommendation systems can monitor patient data in real time using wearable devices or remote monitoring systems and recommend interventions before a condition exacerbates. This proactive approach can reduce hospital readmissions and emergency room visits, significantly lowering healthcare costs and improving patient quality of life.

Case Studies: Success Stories in Healthcare

Predictive Analytics in Hospital Readmissions: A notable hospital utilized a recommendation system that analyzed historical patient data to identify those at high risk of readmission. By targeting these patients with personalized follow-up care and intervention plans, the hospital was able to significantly reduce readmission rates, showcasing the potential of data-driven recommendations in improving patient outcomes.

Personalized Cancer Therapy: A leading cancer research center developed a recommendation system that used genomic sequencing data to suggest customized therapy plans for cancer patients. This system was instrumental in identifying effective treatment options for patients who had not responded to standard treatments, highlighting the transformative potential of personalized medicine.

Ethical Considerations and the Path Forward

While healthcare recommendation systems offer immense benefits, they also raise important ethical considerations, particularly regarding data privacy and the potential for algorithmic bias. Ensuring the security of patient data and implementing robust algorithms that are transparent and free from bias are crucial challenges that must be addressed as these systems become more widespread.

The future of healthcare recommendation systems is promising, with advances in AI, machine learning, and genomics driving continuous innovation. Integrating natural language processing could further enhance these systems, enabling them to interpret doctors' notes and patient feedback to refine recommendations.

Finance

In the dynamic realm of finance, recommendation systems have emerged as transformative tools, enabling financial institutions to deliver highly personalized services to their clients. By harnessing the power of data analytics and sophisticated

algorithms, these systems can sift through vast amounts of financial data to identify investment opportunities, products, and services that align closely with each client's unique risk profile, economic history, and long-term goals.

Personalized Financial Guidance

The essence of financial recommendation systems lies in their ability to provide personalized advice, moving beyond generic suggestions to offer insights and recommendations that are genuinely tailored to the individual. For instance, a client looking to invest may have a specific risk tolerance, investment timeframe, and financial goals. A recommendation system can analyze this client's past investment behavior, current economic status, and broader market trends to suggest a portfolio that maximizes returns while adhering to the client's risk appetite.

Enhancing Investment Strategies

These systems can play a pivotal role in the investment domain by informing clients of market opportunities that fit their investment strategies. By constantly monitoring market conditions and analyzing historical data, these systems can identify trends and predict potential market movements, suggesting timely investment actions like buying, holding, or selling assets.

For example, a client with a conservative investment profile might be recommended for bonds or stable dividend-paying stocks. In contrast, a more aggressive investor might receive recommendations for high-growth tech stocks or emerging market opportunities. This level of customization ensures that each client's portfolio is optimized for their specific circumstances, leading to better financial outcomes.

Streamlining Product Offerings

Beyond investment advice, financial recommendation systems are adept at matching clients with the most suitable financial products, whether the correct type of savings account, loan, credit card, or insurance policy. By analyzing a client's economic activity, credit history, and personal preferences, these systems can suggest products that meet the client's current needs and offer the best terms and rates.

For instance, a recommendation system might suggest a credit card with travel benefits to a client who frequently makes international transactions or a high-yield savings account to a client with a growing balance in a standard account, thus enhancing client satisfaction and loyalty.

Success Stories: Transforming Finance with AI

Robo-Advisors in Wealth Management: Robo-advisors represent one of the most successful applications of recommendation systems in finance. These automated platforms provide personalized investment management services, using algorithms to build and manage a diversified portfolio based on the client's risk tolerance and investment goals. Firms like Betterment and Wealthfront have successfully leveraged this technology to democratize investment advice, making it accessible and affordable.

Credit Scoring and Loan Approval: Financial institutions increasingly use recommendation systems to improve their credit scoring models. By analyzing a more comprehensive range of data, including non-traditional sources like rental payment histories or utility bills, these systems can offer more accurate creditworthiness assessments, leading to more personalized loan and credit offerings.

Navigating Ethical and Regulatory Landscapes

Deploying recommendation systems in finance has challenges, particularly regarding ethical considerations and regulatory compliance. Ensuring the privacy and security of client data is paramount, as is the need to avoid biased or discriminatory recommendations. Financial institutions must navigate these challenges carefully, ensuring their recommendation systems are transparent, fair, and fully compliant with financial regulations.

The Future of Finance with Recommendation Systems

Looking ahead, the role of recommendation systems in finance is set to expand further, with emerging technologies like blockchain and quantum computing poised to enhance their capabilities. As these systems become more advanced, they can offer more nuanced recommendations, anticipate client needs more effectively, and contribute to more robust financial planning and decision-making processes.

Education

In education, the advent of recommendation systems has marked a significant paradigm shift, enabling a more personalized and adaptive learning experience. These systems, leveraging sophisticated algorithms, are adept at parsing vast datasets to offer tailored educational content, be it courses, readings, or activities, that align with individual students' learning styles, academic performance, and personal interests. This level of personalization fosters a more engaging and effective educational journey, potentially transforming the outcomes for learners.

Tailoring Education to Individual Needs

The foundation of educational recommendation systems is understanding and catering to each learner's unique needs. By analyzing data points such as past academic performance, course preferences, engagement levels in various subjects, and even time spent on topics, these systems can identify the most suitable learning materials and courses for each student. For instance, a student struggling with mathematics might receive recommendations for resources focusing on foundational concepts in a visual and interactive format that matches their learning style.

Enhancing Engagement and Retention

One critical benefit of recommendation systems in education is their ability to boost student engagement significantly. By providing students with relevant and challenging content, these systems can maintain students' interest and motivation levels. For example, an online learning platform might suggest a coding course to a student who has shown an aptitude for mathematics and expressed interest in video games, thereby aligning educational content with the student's passions and strengths.

Moreover, such personalized recommendations can also aid in retention, especially in online learning environments where dropout rates are a concern. Tailored learning paths that adapt to a student's progress ensure that the material remains accessible yet challenging, reducing frustration and the likelihood of disengagement.

Supporting Diverse Learning Paths

Educational recommendation systems offer diverse, flexible learning paths accommodating learners' paces and styles. Students who quickly grasp new concepts might be directed towards more advanced topics or accelerated programs. At the same time, another might receive additional resources on challenging subjects, ensuring that each learner can progress at a pace that suits them best.

Furthermore, these systems can introduce interdisciplinary learning opportunities, recommending courses or materials that bridge different subjects based on a student's interests and performance. For example, a student excelling in environmental science and political studies might receive recommendations for courses in environmental policy, fostering a multidisciplinary approach to learning.

Real-World Success Stories

Adaptive Learning Platforms: Platforms like Khan Academy and Coursera have successfully integrated recommendation systems to offer personalized learning experiences. By analyzing user interactions and performance on quizzes and assignments, these platforms can recommend specific videos, exercises, and courses tailored to the user's learning trajectory, enhancing understanding and mastery of subjects.

University Course Recommendations: Several universities have implemented recommendation systems to assist students in course selection, considering their academic history, career aspirations, and elective preferences. This has streamlined the course selection process and ensured that students choose courses that align with their academic goals and interests, leading to more satisfying educational experiences.

Ethical Considerations and Future Prospects

While recommendation systems hold immense promise for personalized education, they also raise ethical considerations, particularly regarding data privacy and the potential for algorithmic bias. Safeguarding student data and ensuring that recommendations are fair and unbiased are paramount for the ethical deployment of these systems.

Integrating emerging technologies like AI and natural language processing could further refine the capabilities of educational recommendation systems. Future systems could analyze student essays and open-ended responses to gain deeper insights into students' comprehension and interests, offering even more nuanced and practical recommendations.

Managerial Insights

For managers considering the adoption of recommendation systems, the key lies in understanding their industry's unique needs and dynamics. Here are some actionable insights.

- **Data is Key**: The effectiveness of a recommendation system is directly tied to the quality and quantity of data available. Ensuring comprehensive data collection and management processes is crucial.

- **User Experience**: The primary goal of a recommendation system should be to enhance the user experience. Recommendations should be relevant, timely, and personalized.
- **Ethical Considerations**: It's essential to consider the ethical implications of recommendation systems, particularly regarding data privacy and bias. Transparent data practices and regular audits can help mitigate these concerns.
- **Continuous Improvement**: Recommendation systems should not be static. To maintain effectiveness, they must constantly analyze and refine themselves based on user feedback and changing trends.
- **Cross-Disciplinary Teams**: Implementing a successful recommendation system often requires a cross-disciplinary team that includes data scientists, industry experts, and UX designers, ensuring that the system is not only technically sound but also aligned with business goals and user needs.

Conclusion

Recommendation systems offer vast potential across industries to personalize the user experience, streamline content discovery, and drive business growth. Managers can harness this technology to gain a competitive edge in the digital marketplace by understanding the principles behind these systems and their successful applications.

6. The Current Landscape and Future Trends

We now delve into the current state-of-the-art technologies and methodologies that underpin recommendation systems, exploring how advancements in artificial intelligence (AI), machine learning (ML), and deep learning are reshaping these systems. We also examine the integration of cutting-edge technologies like blockchain, augmented reality (AR), and virtual reality (VR) and speculate on the future directions and potential impacts of recommendation systems on various industries.

State of the Art in Recommendation Systems

The landscape of recommendation systems has undergone significant transformation with the advent of Artificial Intelligence (AI) and Machine Learning (ML), mainly through deep learning techniques. These state-of-the-art methodologies have expanded the capabilities of recommendation systems and improved their precision, making them indispensable tools in various sectors, from e-commerce and entertainment to healthcare and education.

Deep Learning: The Game Changer in Recommendations

Deep learning, a sophisticated branch of ML, employs neural networks with multiple layers (hence "deep") to analyze vast amounts of data. These neural networks, inspired by the structure of the human brain, have dramatically enhanced the ability of recommendation systems to recognize intricate patterns and predict user preferences with remarkable accuracy.

- **Convolutional Neural Networks (CNNs):** CNNs are particularly adept at processing image data, making them valuable for recommendation systems in platforms that rely heavily on visual content, such as fashion e-commerce or social media. For example, Pinterest uses CNNs to analyze the visual content of pins. By understanding the features of images that users interact with, Pinterest

can recommend visually similar pins, enhancing user engagement and content discovery.
- **Recurrent Neural Networks (RNNs):** RNNs handle sequential data, making them ideal for platforms where the order of interactions matters, such as music or video streaming services. Spotify, for instance, employs RNNs to understand users' listening sequences, enabling the platform to recommend songs or playlists that match the user's musical taste and complement their listening journey, maintaining a coherent and enjoyable listening experience.

Real-Life Applications of Advanced Recommendation Systems

Netflix's Personalized Recommendations: Netflix, a pioneer in personalized content delivery, leverages deep learning algorithms to analyze users' viewing histories, search patterns, and even the time spent on each title. This analysis helps Netflix recommend shows and movies that match individual users' tastes, significantly enhancing user satisfaction and retention.

The recommendation engine is so pivotal to Netflix's success that the company once offered a million-dollar prize to anyone who could improve its recommendation algorithm by 10%.

Amazon's Product Recommendations: Amazon's recommendation system, famously known as "item-to-item collaborative filtering," has set a benchmark in the e-commerce industry. It personalizes the shopping experience by suggesting products based on the user's browsing history, purchase history, and items in their shopping cart. Deep learning algorithms allow Amazon to continually refine these recommendations, ensuring they remain relevant and compelling, increasing cross-selling and upselling opportunities.

The Impact of Advanced Algorithms on User Experience

The sophistication of modern recommendation systems lies in their ability to analyze historical data, predict future preferences, and adapt to changing user behaviors in real-time. This dynamic adaptability ensures that recommendations remain relevant, enhancing the user experience and fostering a deeper connection between users and platforms.

For instance, YouTube's recommendation system analyzes billions of data points to suggest videos that keep users engaged on the platform for longer durations. It considers the user's past viewing history and factors like watch time, likes, and dislikes, ensuring that the recommended content is similar and of interest to the user.

Ethical Considerations and Future Directions

As recommendation systems become more ingrained in our digital experiences, ethical considerations, particularly concerning data privacy and algorithmic bias, become paramount. Ensuring these systems operate transparently and somewhat is paramount to maintaining user trust and avoiding unintended consequences.

Integrating emerging technologies such as Generative Adversarial Networks (GANs) and reinforcement learning could further enhance the capabilities of recommendation systems. GANs, for instance, could generate new content based on user preferences, while reinforcement learning could optimize recommendations based on real-time user feedback, opening new frontiers in personalized digital experiences.

Integrating with New Technologies

Integrating recommendation systems with new technologies such as blockchain, augmented reality (AR), and virtual reality (VR) is paving the way for innovative applications across various industries. These technologies are enhancing the capabilities of recommendation systems and redefining user experiences, making them more immersive, secure, and personalized.

Blockchain: Enhancing Trust and Security

Blockchain technology, known for its decentralized and tamper-proof ledger, brings new transparency and security to recommendation systems, particularly in handling and storing user data. By leveraging blockchain, recommendation systems can record user interactions and preferences on a secure, immutable ledger, enhancing trust in the system's recommendations.

> **Real-Life Example: Music Streaming Services** Consider a music streaming service that uses blockchain to record users' listening habits, song ratings, and playlist creations. This decentralized approach ensures the integrity of the data and allows for transparent and fair recommendations, free from manipulation by the service provider or third parties. As a result, users can trust that the recommendations are genuinely based on their preferences and the collective insights from the user community.

Augmented Reality (AR): Creating Immersive Experiences

AR technology transforms recommendation systems by providing users with immersive experiences that enhance engagement and satisfaction. By overlaying digital information in the real world, AR enables users to visualize products or content in context, making recommendations more tangible and relatable.

Real-Life Example: IKEA Place App

IKEA's Place app is a prime example of how AR can be integrated into recommendation systems. The app allows users to visualize how furniture and home products would look in their own space before purchasing. By recommending products based on the user's room dimensions and style preferences, the app personalizes the shopping experience and reduces the uncertainty and hesitation often associated with online furniture shopping.

Virtual Reality (VR): Revolutionizing Retail and Real Estate

VR technology is taking recommendation systems to new heights by offering fully immersive experiences. In sectors like retail and real estate, VR can transport users to virtual environments where they can explore products, properties, and spaces in a highly interactive and lifelike manner.

Real-Life Example: Real Estate Virtual Tours

In the real estate sector, VR-based recommendation systems can offer potential buyers virtual tours of properties. These systems can recommend properties based on the buyer's preferences, such as location, budget, and design aesthetics, and then provide a virtual walkthrough of shortlisted properties. This makes the property search process more efficient and allows buyers to get a realistic feel of the space, aiding in their decision-making process.

Real-Life Example: Virtual Dressing Rooms

Virtual dressing rooms powered by VR technology enhance the online shopping experience in retail. Users can try on clothes virtually, seeing how different outfits look on their avatars. This immersive experience, combined with personalized recommendations based on the user's size, style preferences, and past purchases, significantly improves user engagement and reduces return rates.

Ethical Considerations and Future Directions

As recommendation systems integrate with blockchain, AR, and VR, ethical considerations, particularly data privacy and user consent, become increasingly important. Ensuring that users know and consent to how their data is used and stored is crucial in maintaining trust and fostering a positive user experience.

The potential for integrating recommendation systems with emerging technologies is vast. The advent of 5G, with its high-speed and low-latency capabilities, is set to enhance further the performance and responsiveness of AR and VR applications, making real-time personalized recommendations even more seamless and engaging.

As we look toward the future, it's clear that recommendation systems will continue to evolve, becoming more integrated into our daily lives and business operations. The use of AI and ML will deepen, with systems becoming more autonomous in learning and adapting to user preferences. Integrating natural language processing (NLP) will enable systems to understand and process user queries and feedback more effectively, making recommendations even more personalized and context-aware.

The potential for hyper-personalization through the Internet of Things (IoT) is a notable future direction. IoT devices can provide real-time data streams that feed into recommendation systems, enabling highly personalized and situational recommendations. For instance, a smart refrigerator could recommend recipes based on the ingredients it detects inside, coupled with the user's dietary preferences and past cooking habits.

Blockchain's role in ensuring data privacy and security in recommendation systems is expected to grow, addressing growing concerns around data misuse and privacy violations. Meanwhile, AR and VR technologies could revolutionize the retail and entertainment industries by offering highly immersive and interactive experiences based on personalized recommendations.

Potential Impact on Businesses

The advancements in recommendation systems hold significant implications for businesses across sectors. In retail, hyper-personalized and immersive shopping experiences could increase customer engagement and conversion rates. In healthcare, AI-driven recommendations could lead to more accurate diagnoses and personalized treatment plans, improving patient outcomes. In education, adaptive learning systems could offer customized learning paths for students, enhancing learning efficiency and outcomes.

However, these advancements also present challenges, particularly in data privacy, ethical AI use, and the potential for systemic biases in recommendation algorithms. Businesses must navigate these challenges carefully, ensuring their recommendation systems are transparent, fair, and aligned with ethical standards.

Conclusion

Recommendation systems are set to become more sophisticated, integrated, and impactful in the coming years. Understanding these systems' current capabilities and future directions is crucial for managers and business professionals to leverage them to drive innovation, enhance customer experiences, and maintain a competitive edge in the rapidly evolving digital landscape.

7. Implementing Recommendation Systems in Your Organization

Now, we will discuss implementing recommendation systems within an organization. It addresses the initial steps of getting started, navigating potential challenges, and measuring success to ensure continuous improvement and alignment with business objectives.

Getting Started with Recommendation Systems

Implementing a recommendation system begins with setting precise goals, understanding the data landscape, and assembling a skilled team. This foundational phase lays the groundwork for developing a system that aligns with your organization's specific needs and objectives, ensuring successful integration and impactful outcomes.

Goal Setting

The first step in implementing a recommendation system is to define clear, achievable goals. Your role in this is crucial. Identify the specific business needs or problems the recommendation system is intended to address, such as improving user engagement, increasing sales through personalized product recommendations, or enhancing content discovery on a platform.

Data Requirements

Understanding and gathering the necessary data is crucial—it's a responsibility. Data can range from user behavior analytics, such as clicks, views, and purchase history, to product or content metadata. Ensuring data quality and relevance is paramount for the recommendation system's effectiveness.

Team Composition

Assembling the right team is vital for successfully developing and deploying a recommendation system. The team should include data scientists skilled in ML and AI, data engineers handling data infrastructure, UI/UX designers integrating recommendations seamlessly into the user experience, and project managers overseeing the implementation process.

Overcoming Challenges

Navigating the intricate landscape of implementing recommendation systems involves addressing data privacy, technological complexities, and integration hurdles. This section delves into strategies for overcoming these challenges, ensuring a smooth and compliant integration of recommendation systems into your organization's existing framework.

Data Privacy Concerns

With the increasing scrutiny of data privacy and regulation compliance (e.g., GDPR), ensuring user data is handled ethically and transparently is a significant challenge. Implementing robust data governance policies and transparent user consent mechanisms can help navigate these concerns.

Technological Complexities

The technical intricacies of developing and deploying recommendation systems, from choosing suitable algorithms to scaling the infrastructure, can be daunting. Leveraging existing frameworks and platforms and considering cloud-based solutions can simplify these complexities.

Integration with Existing System

Seamlessly integrating the recommendation system with the existing IT infrastructure and ensuring compatibility with legacy systems can pose challenges. Adopting microservices architecture and APIs can facilitate smoother integration.

Measuring Success

Measuring the success of a recommendation system is a dynamic and ongoing process. Let us explore the need for setting effective KPIs, conducting thorough evaluations, and adopting a culture of continuous improvement. These practices are pivotal in ensuring the recommendation system remains aligned with organizational goals and user expectations, driving meaningful outcomes.

Key Performance Indicators (KPIs)

Establishing KPIs is essential to measuring the recommendation system's effectiveness. Common KPIs include conversion rates, click-through rates, user engagement metrics, and revenue impact. These metrics directly correlate with the recommendation system's initial goals.

Conducting Evaluations

It is crucial to regularly evaluate the recommendation system's performance through A/B testing, user feedback, and data analysis. These evaluations can provide insights into what's working and what needs refinement.

Iteration and Continuous Improvement

Recommendation systems should not be static; they must evolve with changing user preferences and

behaviors. Continuously iterating based on evaluation results and emerging trends ensures the system remains practical and relevant.

Real-Life Example: Netflix

Netflix's recommendation system exemplifies successful implementation. The company continually refines its algorithms based on vast amounts of user data, from viewing habits to ratings, to personalize user content. Netflix's investment in A/B testing and machine learning innovation, coupled with its attention to user privacy and data handling, underscores the fundamental principles outlined in this chapter.

Managerial Insights

Managers should approach the implementation of recommendation systems with a strategic mindset, focusing on precise goal setting, thorough planning, and continuous evaluation. Understanding the challenges and potential pitfalls, from data privacy issues to technological hurdles, and adopting best practices can significantly enhance the chances of success. Ultimately, the goal is to leverage recommendation systems as strategic tools to improve user experiences, drive business growth, and maintain a competitive edge in the market.

Conclusion

This chapter serves as a comprehensive guide for managers looking to harness the power of recommendation systems. By following the outlined steps, addressing challenges proactively, and focusing on continuous improvement, organizations can unlock the full potential of recommendation systems to achieve their business objectives.

8. Ethical Considerations and Best Practices

In an era where data is the new oil, recommendation systems stand at the forefront of technological innovation, driving personalized user experiences across various digital platforms. However, with great power comes great responsibility. This chapter delves into the ethical use of data, strategies to mitigate bias in recommendation algorithms, and a compilation of best practices for managing recommendation systems, ensuring they serve the greater good while propelling business objectives forward.

We have discussed these topics in parts in the previous chapters. Now, we put them all together.

Ethical Use of Data

The cornerstone of ethical data use in recommendation systems lies in transparency, consent, and privacy. Users must be informed about what data is collected and how it's used and have

control over their information. A case in point is Spotify, which transparently communicates its data practices and offers users granular privacy settings, allowing them to tailor their data-sharing preferences. This approach builds trust and aligns with regulatory frameworks like the GDPR, setting a benchmark for ethical data use in recommendation systems.

Mitigating Bias

Bias in recommendation algorithms can skew results, perpetuating stereotypes or marginalizing certain groups. To counter this, employing diverse datasets and continuously auditing algorithms for bias is crucial. Pinterest, for example, has made strides in eliminating bias in its recommendation system by diversifying the data fed into its algorithms, ensuring a wide range of interests and perspectives are represented. This commitment to fairness enhances user experience and broadens the platform's appeal.

Best Practices

Managing recommendation systems ethically, legally, and operationally involves a multifaceted approach.

1. **Transparency and User Control**: Communicate data practices and give users control over their data, like Netflix's transparent ratings system, which feeds into its recommendations.
2. **Diverse Data Sources**: Ensure the data used to train algorithms is varied and representative, avoiding biases arising from homogenous datasets.
3. **Continuous Monitoring and Auditing**: Regularly audit recommendation algorithms for accuracy, fairness, and unintended consequences, employing third-party audits for an unbiased review.
4. **User Feedback Loops**: Incorporate user feedback to refine and adjust recommendations, ensuring they remain relevant and respectful of user preferences.
5. **Compliance and Legal Considerations**: Follow and comply with all relevant data

protection and privacy laws, adapting practices as regulations evolve.
6. **Ethical AI Practices**: Adopt ethical AI guidelines that govern the development and deployment of recommendation systems, focusing on fairness, accountability, and transparency.
7. **Cross-functional Teams**: Foster collaboration between data scientists, legal advisors, ethicists, and user experience designers to ensure a holistic approach to recommendation system management.

Conclusion

As recommendation systems become increasingly integral to digital experiences, the imperative to manage them responsibly cannot be overstated. By adhering to ethical practices, actively working to eliminate bias, and embracing a set of best practices grounded in transparency and user respect, managers can harness the power of recommendation systems to drive business success while upholding the highest ethical standards. This chapter guides managers in navigating the complex landscape of recommendation systems, ensuring their use benefits the business and the broader society.

9. Rounding it up

As we conclude this exploration of Recommendation Systems, we must reflect on the transformative journey we've embarked upon. From the nascent stages of manual suggestions to today's sophisticated, AI-driven systems, recommendation technologies have evolved dramatically, becoming indispensable in shaping user experiences and driving business success.

Recap and Reflection

The journey began with understanding the evolution of recommendation systems, tracing their roots from basic manual suggestions to the complex algorithms that define them today. The narrative then transitioned to understanding the core principles that underpin these systems, including personalization, user profiles, and item cataloging, all crafted with minimal mathematical complexity to cater to a diverse managerial audience.

The narrative deepened by exploring time series and market basket analysis, unveiling the intricacies of leveraging temporal patterns and item associations to refine recommendation accuracy. This was complemented by vivid illustrations from various industries, from entertainment to e-commerce, healthcare, finance, and education, showcasing recommendation systems' broad applicability and transformative potential.

Emerging trends and technologies like AI, ML, blockchain, AR, and VR were examined, highlighting innovative integrations that set new benchmarks in personalization and user engagement. The discussion on implementing recommendation systems provided pragmatic insights into initiating projects, overcoming challenges, and measuring success, equipping managers with the knowledge to navigate the deployment complexities.

Finally, the discourse on ethical considerations and best practices emphasized the importance of ethical data use, bias mitigation, and adherence to legal frameworks, ensuring that the deployment of recommendation systems aligns with ethical standards and societal values.

Call to Action

The insights gleaned from each chapter underscore the pivotal role of recommendation systems in the modern business landscape. These systems are not mere technological tools but strategic assets that can drive innovation, enhance customer experiences, and create a competitive edge.

Regardless of their technical background, managers are encouraged to embrace the potential of recommendation systems within their organizations. The opportunities are boundless, whether improving product discoverability on an e-commerce platform, personalizing content on a streaming service, or enhancing patient care in healthcare settings.

Embracing the Future

The future of recommendation systems is ripe with possibilities. As technologies continue to advance, integrating AI, blockchain, AR, VR, and other emerging technologies will unlock new frontiers in personalization and user engagement. Managers who stay abreast of these developments and leverage the insights provided in this book will be well-equipped to

lead their organizations into a future where recommendation systems are a cornerstone of business strategy.

In this age of information and innovation, let recommendation systems be your guide to unlocking new opportunities, fostering deeper connections with your users, and driving your organization toward unparalleled success. The journey into the realm of recommendation systems is just beginning, and the path ahead is full of potential. Embrace it with open arms and an eager spirit; the future is yours to shape.

About the Author

Partha Majumdar is just a programmer.

Partha has a passion for sharing knowledge. He documents his experiences in technical and management aspects in his blog, http://www.parthamajumdar.org. He also regularly publishes videos on his YouTube channel, https://www.youtube.com/channel/UCbzrZ_aeyiYVo1WJKhIP5sQ.

Partha has continued to learn new domains and technology throughout his career. After graduating in Mathematics, Partha completed a master's in Telecommunications, a master's in Computer Security, and a master's in Information Technology. He has also completed two Executive MBAs in Information Systems and Business Analytics. He completed a PG Certificate program in AI/ML/DL from Manipal Academy of Higher Education (Dubai), an advanced certificate in Cyber Security from IIT (Kanpur), and a PG-level advanced certificate in Computational Data Sciences from IISc (Bengaluru). He is pursuing a Doctorate in Business Administration from the Swiss School of Business and Management (Geneva).

Books by the Author

Learn Emotion Analysis with R

This book is a comprehensive guide to Emotion Analysis using Lexicons, offering a step-by-step code walkthrough for developing Sentiment and Emotion Analysis systems with data from WhatsApp and Twitter. It introduces R and Shiny programming, essential for building emotion analysis systems. The discussion then extends to the fundamentals of Sentiment and Emotion Analysis, leading to the creation of Shiny applications tailored for this purpose. The book concludes by developing a specialized tool for analyzing emotions from Twitter and WhatsApp data. Additionally, it hints at advancing into Machine Learning for Emotion Analysis, contingent on the availability of labeled data, positioning this as a subsequent step for readers.

Link in Amazon Store: https://www.amazon.com/dp/B096K2SVF2

Mastering Classification Algorithms for Machine Learning

This book delves into the core of machine learning through the lens of classification algorithms, which play a pivotal role in categorizing input based on its features. These algorithms are the backbone of various applications, from spam detection to fraud prevention. Starting with a foundational overview of problem-solving in machine learning, the book transitions to a focused examination of classification challenges. It provides an in-depth exploration of the Naïve Bayes algorithm, Logistic Regression, including the crucial sigmoid function, and Decision Trees, highlighting key concepts like the Gini Factor and Entropy. Furthermore, it elaborates on the Random Forest algorithm and concludes with an insightful discussion on Boosting techniques, offering a comprehensive guide to mastering classification algorithms in machine learning.

Link in Amazon Store: https://www.amazon.com/dp/935551851X

Machine Learning for Managers

"Machine Learning for Managers" is a comprehensive guide tailored for leaders aiming to leverage machine learning (ML) within their organizations. It simplifies ML concepts, emphasizing strategic applications over technical complexity. The book covers integrating ML into business practices, ethical data use, and real-world industry applications, showcasing ML's role in enhancing operations and innovation. It also provides insights on team building in the ML era, promoting cross-disciplinary collaboration for effective ML adoption. This book is a strategic roadmap for managers to harness ML, driving informed decision-making and positioning their organizations for future success in an AI-driven landscape.

Link in Amazon Store: https://www.amazon.in/dp/B0CZ5XTQ1L

Deep Learning for Managers

"Deep Learning for Managers" is a pivotal guide for modern leaders navigating the AI revolution. It demystifies deep learning, making it accessible to managers without requiring deep technical knowledge. This book equips leaders with the insights to harness AI effectively, covering everything from the basics of artificial neural networks to the ethical considerations of AI deployment. It's an indispensable resource for any leader aiming to leverage deep learning as a strategic asset in today's rapidly evolving business landscape.

Link in Amazon Store: https://www.amazon.in/dp/B0CWDPWSN8

Generative AI for Managers

"Generative AI for Managers" is a cutting-edge guide that demystifies Generative AI for business leaders eager to harness this technology for growth and innovation. It delves into how Generative AI can revolutionize aspects of business, from enhancing customer experiences to optimizing operations and driving strategic decision-making. The book provides a wealth of practical applications, showcases how mundane tasks can be automated for efficiency, and presents strategies for fostering a culture of innovation through AI. Additionally, it offers guidance on the ethical implementation of AI technologies, ensuring they complement and augment human capabilities within the organizational framework, thereby paving the way for a future rich in opportunities and advancements.

Link in Amazon Store: https://www.amazon.in/dp/B0CXYBFJHD

ChatGPT AI for Managers

"ChatGPT for Managers" is a vital resource for leaders navigating the AI revolution, focusing on integrating Generative AI, like ChatGPT, in enhancing managerial functions and team dynamics. It provides practical insights into leveraging ChatGPT to streamline tasks, bolster decision-making, and encourage innovative thinking within teams. This guide transcends theoretical knowledge, offering actionable strategies for managers to complement their skills with AI, thereby elevating their leadership effectiveness. Through real-world applications and expert advice, readers will learn to harmonize traditional management with AI advancements, ensuring they remain at the forefront of the evolving business environment.

Link in Amazon Store: https://www.amazon.in/dp/B0CY8L4CQ9

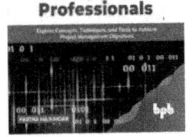

Linear Programming for Project Management Professionals

This guide equips project management professionals with strategies to address project crashing through linear programming, ensuring timely completion and cost efficiency. It starts with foundational project management concepts and progresses to monitoring techniques and linear programming problem (LPP) formulation. The book delves into solving LPPs, highlighting the use of tools like Microsoft Excel's Solver. It offers insights into applying these methods to real-world project crashing scenarios, emphasizing time and cost optimization. Additionally, it explores the integration of earned value management in project crashing, providing a

comprehensive toolkit for project management teams to navigate complex project challenges.

Link in Amazon Store: https://www.amazon.com/dp/B09PD1GFMY

Mutual Fund Investing

"Mutual Fund Investing" is a definitive guide designed specifically for middle-class investors in India and beyond, simplifying the intricate world of mutual funds. It thoroughly explains mutual funds, including their types and the critical differences between open-ended and closed funds. The book offers strategic insights into systematic investments, tax implications, and the balance of benefits and drawbacks. It guides readers through assessing risk tolerance, interpreting crucial financial metrics, and making well-informed investment choices. Advanced techniques like Piotrowski's F-Score and Mohanram's G-Score equip investors to build diversified portfolios, evaluate fund performance, and refine their investment strategies. Tailored for beginners and seasoned investors, this book is essential for anyone looking to achieve financial growth and security through mutual funds.

Link in Amazon Store: https://www.amazon.com/dp/B0CYNG6B12

Creating an Investment Portfolio

This book delves into the scientific process of making informed investment decisions, highlighting the importance for individuals and corporations. It explores critical theories and applications in portfolio creation, covering various investment vehicles like fixed deposits, mutual funds, and shares, emphasizing the necessary mathematics. Additionally, it introduces simple yet widely used tools for investment calculations. Designed to be accessible to a broad audience, this book is an invaluable guide for beginners and experienced investors aiming to enhance their understanding and effectiveness in investing.

Link in Amazon Store: https://www.amazon.com/dp/B0CK99SPKZ

Gartner Research Analysis

The book provides a clear framework for leveraging insights from the Gartner Hype-Cycle Report, an essential resource for understanding technological trends. It simplifies identifying and evaluating emerging technologies, their developers, and market readiness. A live case study illustrates practical application while emphasizing the need for comprehensive research beyond the report. Essential for those seeking strategic technological guidance, this book demystifies the complex data presented in the Gartner Hype Cycle.

Link in Amazon Store: https://www.amazon.com/dp/B0CK582Y2M

Essay on the Indian Knowledge System – Part 1

The book delves into the Indian Knowledge System (IKS), a comprehensive approach to compiling, conserving, and disseminating India's rich knowledge heritage across various disciplines such as science, mathematics, social sciences, medicine, philosophy, art, and spirituality. It highlights the global perspective of IKS and its relevance in sharing India's intellectual legacy with the world. The study of Indology, or "Bharatatattva," as it's known in Indian scholarship, further explores the historical, cultural, linguistic, and literary facets of the Indian subcontinent. Through a series of concise essays, this book, one of a trilogy on ancient India, offers insights into Bharatatattva, underscoring India's significant contributions to global knowledge.

Link in Amazon Store: https://www.amazon.com/dp/B0CXNN95TR

Corporate Lessons I Learned

This book encapsulates 34 years of corporate experiences up to 2023, presenting a collection of impactful incidents and interactions that shaped the author's career. Primarily aimed at middle and lower-level managers, it offers humorous and insightful recollections that serve as practical guidelines for navigating daily challenges in the corporate world. The author illustrates valuable lessons learned through various encounters, making it a helpful resource for understanding and excelling in corporate management.

Link in Amazon Store: https://www.amazon.in/dp/B0CL3YBSF8

Weekend in Jordan

To celebrate their 20th wedding anniversary, the authors embarked on a spontaneous trip to Jordan, making travel arrangements just a week prior. The feasibility of this last-minute adventure was greatly aided by Jordan's visa-on-arrival policy for Indians and many other nationalities, making it an accessible destination for a broad audience. Their weekend in Jordan was filled with memorable experiences, like being in a movie, with the country's stunning beauty leaving a lasting impression. Despite its modest size, Jordan's rich offerings, from Petra's historical wonders to the Dead Sea's unique allure and Amman's vibrant city life, were thoroughly explored. This book recounts their remarkable journey, offering insights into the treasures of Jordan.

Link in Amazon Store: https://www.amazon.com/dp/B0CK5N6B3W

Elephant Ride in Chang Wangpo

In 2022, Thailand saw a significant influx of approximately 11.5 million tourists, underlining tourism's vital role in its economy, contributing around 6% to the Thai GDP. Reflecting on their past residency in Bangkok from 1996 to 1999, the authors seized a chance to revisit Thailand in 2018, noticing considerable changes. An efficient metro system has alleviated the once notorious Bangkok traffic, enhancing city navigation. While many cherished aspects remained, improvements in the road network and increased attractions enriched their experience. Coinciding with their 26th wedding anniversary, the business trip also included leisure exploration in

Bangkok and Kanchanaburi, with a memorable visit to Chang Wangpo, blending nostalgia, discovery, and celebration.

Link in Amazon Store: https://www.amazon.com/dp/B0CKGWH97S

Weekend in South Sikkim

This book offers an insightful exploration into the less-traveled South Sikkim, diverging from the usual tourist trails in North Sikkim, like Gangtok and Nathu La Pass. The authors journey through various captivating destinations, including Tsomgo Lake, Baba Ka Mandir, and the picturesque Temi Tea Gardens. They delve into the cultural and spiritual essence of South Sikkim with visits to Namchi's Char Dham and Samdruptse Monastery, providing a comprehensive overview of the region's diverse attractions. Additionally, the narrative extends to Yangang and the Bengal Safari in Siliguri, West Bengal, enriching the travelogue with varied experiences.

Link in Amazon Store: https://www.amazon.com/dp/B0CKL1DNTJ

Trips to Dubai

This travelogue unveils the multifaceted allure of Dubai, a top-tier tourist hub known for landmarks like the Burj Khalifa and Burj Al Arab, alongside thrilling experiences such as helicopter rides and dolphin encounters at the Atlantis. It extends beyond Dubai, shedding light on Abu Dhabi and Sharjah attractions, like the adrenaline-pumping Ferrari World and the enchanting Desert Safari. The author shares personal adventures, offering insights into the intricacies of visiting Dubai and navigating the Gulf region, making this book a valuable resource for anyone looking to explore the rich experiences Dubai and its neighboring emirates offer.

Link in Amazon Store: https://www.amazon.com/dp/B0CKRYQKDN

1-Day Trips from Bengaluru

From 1975 to 2023, Bengaluru evolved from a retirees' haven to India's Silicon Valley, also renowned as the Garden City. While Bengaluru has numerous tourist attractions and activity hubs, the city's vicinity offers many exploration destinations. This book focuses on day-trip-worthy spots around Bengaluru, places steeped in historical and mythological significance. It does not cover prominent cities like Mysuru, Chennai, and Hyderabad, as well as scenic locales like Ooty, Goa, and Kerala, as they need more than a day to tour.

Link in Amazon Store: https://www.amazon.com/dp/B0CLK58KTB

A Trip to the Wagah Border

The Wagah Border, straddling India and Pakistan near Amritsar and Lahore, is famed for its ceremonial displays by border forces, symbolizing hope amidst strained relations. This checkpoint, pivotal for prisoner exchanges, represents a unique reconciliation potential. On festive occasions, friendly exchanges between the forces foster harmony. The book visually explores Chandigarh, Shimla, Amritsar, and the Wagah Border, highlighting their rich cultures and historical importance.

Link in Amazon Store: https://www.amazon.com/dp/B0CLYTQ6PV

Weekend Getaways from Bengaluru

This guidebook enhances the tourism experience in India, emphasizing the country's improved accessibility and facilities that cater to all traveler categories. It outlines explicitly short trips from Bengaluru, covering a mix of destinations accessible by road, rail, and air. The book is a resource for planning 2-, 3-, and 4-day excursions to various South Indian locales and select sites in Maharashtra, featuring popular tourist destinations such as Ooty, Kodaikanal, and Mysuru, as well as revered places of worship like Kukke Subramanya and Dharmasthala. It offers practical travel tips, what to anticipate on journeys and insights into each destination's unique offerings.

Link in Amazon Store: https://www.amazon.com/dp/B0CMNRKWQ9

www.ingramcontent.com/pod-product-compliance
Lightning Source LLC
Chambersburg PA
CBHW052211220526
45471CB00004B/1911